How do I use this scheme?

Key Words with Peter and Jane has three
parallel series, each containing twelve books. All three
series are written using the same carefully controlled
vocabulary. Readers will get the most out of **Key Words** with
Peter and Jane when they follow the books in the pattern
1a, 1b, 1c; 2a, 2b, 2c and so on.

• Series a
gradually introduces and repeats new words.

• Series b
provides further practice of these same words, but
in a different context and with different illustrations.

• Series c
uses familiar words to teach **phonics** in a methodical way,
enabling children to read increasingly difficult words.
It also provides a link to writing.

LADYBIRD BOOKS

UK | USA | Canada | Ireland | Australia
India | New Zealand | South Africa

Ladybird Books is part of the Penguin Random House group of companies
whose addresses can be found at global.penguinrandomhouse.com.

www.penguin.co.uk   www.puffin.co.uk   www.ladybird.co.uk

First published 1964
This edition 2009, 2014, 2016
Copyright © Ladybird Books Ltd, 1964
001

A CIP catalogue record for this book is
available from the British Library

ISBN: 978-1-409-30141-7

Printed in China

Key Words
with Peter and Jane

12b Mountain adventure

written by W. Murray
illustrated by M. Aitchison

A year ago, Simon and John stayed at a castle during their holiday. In this castle they found a box of very old documents which were valuable. The owner of the castle and the documents was Mr. Jones, who gave two gold coins to each of the boys as a reward. The gold coins had been found in the same box as the documents and they also were very old and valuable. At the time, the boys asked Mr. Jones if they could sell their gold coins. He told them that the reward was theirs to use as they wished.

During the year, the boys talked many times of selling the coins and spending the money. They had many plans which they discussed with their friends and other people. At last they decided what to do. They sold the gold coins to start a club for young people.

First they found a building large enough for the Club. The owner agreed to let them have it and said they could decorate it themselves. "It will be fun for us to decorate the place," said John to Simon. "Yes," replied his brother. "We must start as soon as possible."

They discussed their ideas with a few of their friends and soon got to work. They started on the largest room.

Their plan was to use this as a gym where they could have sports and games. They could also use the large space for dancing. In one corner they made a coffee bar and a place for a record player. They prepared this corner first so that they could have music to listen to while they worked, and something to drink when they had a rest.

The news of the Club soon spread amongst their friends. Before long, many young people of their own age visited them to see what they were doing. "You can't play records or drink coffee unless you work first," Simon explained to them. "We want to get the Club started as soon as we can. We need more help." They soon got the help they needed and by the end of the fourth week the repairs and decorating of all rooms were finished.

Then came the time to get furniture and equipment. Some of this furniture and equipment was given to the Club by friends. To get the rest of it, they had to spend some more of their money.

"Well," said Simon, "the paint has dried, the furniture has come and the equipment has arrived and been fitted. We're ready to open the Club." He read from a paper on which he had been writing. "The Club has twenty members who have paid their entry fees and there are another twenty five who are expected to join in a few days. I think we can count on having forty five members. We ought to have a meeting." His brother agreed to this. "Yes, there are several things to decide," he said.

A few days later, the meeting was held. Forty two boy and girl members were there, all with plenty to say. The girls promised to make curtains for all the windows and wanted to know if they could cook food in the kitchen. Some boys asked if they could put on a play. Others said that the Club should have a higher entry fee so that they could have money for sports teams. Many other ideas were discussed.

Simon was made the Club leader. He announced that groups would be formed so that the work agreed upon could be carried out.

After the meeting, the coffee bar and the gym were opened for all members.

The Club was now open each evening. More young people became members and soon Simon and John were busy nearly every evening. Most of the boys liked the gym and spent a lot of time there. They climbed the long ropes, and skipped to keep themselves fit. The punchball was used often and many of the bigger boys liked to throw the heavy medicine ball to one another.

The girls did not use the punchball or the medicine ball. Some of them liked to skip and to join the boys in playing basket-ball. Others were often happy to sit in the rest room talking, reading, or making curtains or something else the Club needed. Once a week there was a dance and everyone took part.

The boys who liked a lot of exercise in the gym were always looking for something new to do. Simon and John bought a rowing machine which pleased their friends. Then they got some large mats for judo. These mats were thick and made of rubber, so that anyone who fell on them would not hurt himself. During fine weather many members wanted more exercise outside, and so an Adventure Group was formed.

There were eight boys and four girls in the Adventure Group. They met to discuss what they could do. One of the boys, named Robert, showed the others some colour slides of a holiday he had spent climbing a mountain. Robert said that mountain climbing was very exciting. The one he knew could be climbed on foot from one side. On the other side there was a chair-lift and a cable-car for getting to the top. There was snow on top of the mountain every winter.

The members of the group decided to climb the mountain that their friend knew. First they would do it the easy way, partly on foot and partly by chair-lift and cable-car. Several of them had never had the chance to use a chair-lift or cable-car. Later, they could climb the mountain all the way on foot, from the other side.

Robert explained that they would need strong boots and light but warm clothes for the mountain climb. When they went up on foot they would need a guide to go with them.

A mountain guide is a man used to climbing and who knows a mountain well.

The Adventure Group lost no time in getting ready for the mountain climb. The members were all very excited about it. Then one week-end they set off very early. They went by train a long way, to the foothills leading to the mountain. Here they left the train to start their walk. It was a fine day and they enjoyed the exercise in the fresh air. There were no clouds and they could see the mountain as it lay ahead of them in the sunshine. The top seemed a long way away.

By the afternoon, they reached the lower part of the mountain and the chair-lift. They saw the wires stretching up the mountain side with chairs moving along them. There were several people in the chairs.

Simon and his brother were the first of the Adventure Group to pay their money and to take their seats. The others followed and soon all the members of the group were moving through the air up the mountain side.

"This really is an easy way to do it," said John. "Yes," answered Simon. "It's also a pleasant way of getting a lot of fresh air and sunshine."

Simon and John talked together as they went along on the chair-lift. "What a really wonderful view," said Simon. "Yes," replied John. "We're not very far from the ground, yet we're high enough to see a long way."

The other members of the group were also enjoying themselves. They soon got used to the strange and exciting feeling of moving easily through the air. There was almost no sound as they went along. Everyone thought the view was wonderful.

At the end of the chair-lift there was a station with a long platform which had a roof over it. The platform made it easy for them to get out of their chairs. The members of the Adventure Group collected together round Robert, as he knew what to do next. "Follow me," he said. "There is a little way to walk to the cable-car." He led them along a path and round a pile of large rocks.

They came almost at once to the cable-car station. This was built on a platform on the edge of a deep valley. Above them, the other side of the valley rose steeply towards the mountain top.

Two of the group looked down into the deep valley with alarm. They held on to the handrail round the platform on which they stood. Then they looked upwards at the far side of the valley where it rose steeply towards the mountain top. They could see double cables which stretched from their platform across the valley to a place high above them. "Oh, dear!" said one girl. "Have we got to go up there? I feel afraid."

"So do I," said one of the boys. "Look down into the valley. If by chance the cable broke, that's where we should fall." One of the boys standing near them could hear them talking. "Don't be afraid, it's not dangerous," he said. "The cable is very thick and it won't break. Besides, there is another cable which also holds the car. It is called the safety cable, so even if the first one should break the car would not fall."

All the people waiting paid for their tickets and got into the cable-car. There were no seats, so they all remained standing as the doors closed and the car moved silently upwards. At first nobody spoke.

Most of the boys and girls in the cable-car looked out of the windows as they moved upwards. They could see downwards to the ground far below. Several had a feeling of something like fear, but not one of them showed it to the others. Nobody wanted to look frightened. They began to talk amongst themselves.

Someone had a pair of binoculars and he passed them round so that the others could look down into the valley. There was a path at the bottom and a very small house at the end of it. The people in the cable-car were so far from the house that it looked smaller than a doll's house to them. A tiny figure of a man could be seen walking towards the house. Through the binoculars the tiny animal in front of the man could be seen to be a dog.

It was not long before the cable-car stopped. Their ride was over. They remained in the car until they saw the doors slide open. Then everyone got out of the car to continue the climb to the mountain top.

They went on foot for the rest of the way. It took only a short time.

The boys and girls stood on the top of the mountain for some time. It was a clear day and they had a wonderful view all around them. The binoculars were passed from hand to hand.

A man who was there had been to the mountain top during the winter time. He told the others that it was very cold up there then. There was deep snow on the top during most of the winter months, and little else to see, as very often the mountain top was in a cloud.

The members of the Adventure Group were very interested to see what the other side of the mountain looked like. This was the side they wanted to climb on foot later on. It was not as steep as the one they had just come up by chair-lift and cable-car.

As they looked down the long slopes of the mountain side, they could see that the climb would be difficult. "I can see why we shall need a guide," said Simon to John. "Yes," answered his brother. "We shall have to plan everything carefully. It may take two or three days to climb to the top and go back down again."

They returned to the foot of the mountain, again using the cable-car and the chair-lift. Then they walked to a village where they went to a small café. Next to this café was a shop which sold mountain climbing equipment. Here John bought a book on mountain climbing.

The owner of this shop talked to some of the group about the mountains and mentioned he had a son named Dirk who was a mountain guide in his spare time. "He loves the mountain," he said. "He's never tired of climbing it, and helping others to get to the top. He has done this for years and the exercise has made him strong."

Just then the shopkeeper's son came up. Dirk was a tall young man with clear blue eyes and a smiling face. Simon and the others talked to him and mentioned that they soon intended to climb the mountain for their first time. Dirk was interested at once and before long they had agreed between them that Dirk should be their guide.

It was getting dark as they set off to the station and it was quite late when they arrived at their homes, very tired but happy.

It took nearly a month to make all the arrangements for the week-end mountain climb. They wrote to Dirk and then bought the equipment on the list he sent.

Meanwhile they spent most of their evenings and week-ends at the Club. They enjoyed getting as fit as they could and used the rowing machine and punchball often. Several basket-ball matches were arranged with other clubs. In one of these matches John scored six points. He was the best player in the Club and usually scored some points for his side.

Most of the members of the Club got much pleasure from music. They liked to listen to popular music on records and also to some of the members playing their own instruments. They called the group with their own instruments the 'Pop Group' as it played a lot of popular music. The 'Pop Group' played also at the weekly dance. Tickets were sold for these dances and the money that was made helped to run the Club.

One day Simon found that after all the bills had been paid there was some spare money. With this it was decided to buy a camera to make a film of their week-end visit to the mountain.

The boys and girls were a happy group as they set off on their long week-end trip to the mountain. They expected to enjoy every minute of their trip.

They were glad to meet the smiling Dirk. They had a meal with him before they set off to the foot-hills. While they ate, John asked Dirk if he wanted to be a shopkeeper like his father. "Later on, perhaps," he said. "But while I'm young I intend to live an outdoor life. The longer I'm outdoors, the happier I am. Anyone who lives near a mountain is lucky." He went on to tell them stories about the mountain, and adventures he had had on his climbs.

After the meal they checked their equipment with Dirk and went over the arrangements they had made for the climb. Their guide made them check every piece of equipment carefully. They had light tents with them as they had to spend two nights on the mountain side.

At last they were off up the slopes that led to the mountain. Simon walked last as he had the camera with him and he wanted to make a record of their trip to show the other members of the Club.

They all walked quite quickly at first but slowed down as the road became steeper. After some time, they left the road and took to a mountain path. Dirk led the way along the bank of a pleasant stream which flowed down the mountain side.

Soon they came to a little bridge across the stream. As they walked over the bridge, Dirk told them that they could have a rest. Some of the group sat down on the river bank and ate the sandwiches which they had brought. Meanwhile others stayed on the bridge to look down into the stream. They could see through the clear water to the bottom of the stream.

One of the boys sat down to put his hand into the water. He was surprised that it felt so cold and that it flowed so quickly. His friend pointed to some small fish swimming in the water and then to some coloured stones on the bed of the stream.

Simon climbed on a rock above the bridge and pointed his camera downwards. Then he switched it on to get a shot of the boys by the bridge. He was using colour film in the camera.

When Simon had finished using the camera and when the sandwiches had all gone, Dirk started off again up the mountain side.

They had seen a few mountain sheep on their way, and had heard some of them bleating. Suddenly they heard a very loud bleating as though some of the animals were in trouble. Dirk and the others hurried at once towards the noise.

As they came round a bend in the path, they saw several sheep looking down into a large hole in the rocks. Another sheep had fallen into the hole and could not get out. The boys went to the edge of the hole and looked down into it. At the bottom, a sheep was walking round and round bleating loudly. The sides of the deep hole were very steep, much too steep to be climbed by animal or man.

Everyone saw that the animal could not get out of the deep hole in the rocks, and that if it were left there it would die.

"It's lucky that the sheep has not been badly hurt by its fall," said Dirk. "We must get it out of that hole as soon as possible."

The Adventure Group agreed that the sheep could not be left to die in the deep hole into which it had fallen.

"Don't worry," said Dirk, "I think we can get it out of trouble." He went to a flat rock at the edge of the hole and stood on it. He let down a long rope to the bottom of the hole. He passed the end of the rope he was holding over the overhanging branch of a tree, and then tied it round a very large rock nearby. He pulled on the rope to make sure that it would hold securely. Then he took a piece of canvas from the pack he carried and slid down the rope with it.

Once at the bottom of the hole he made a sling with the canvas and tied it on to the long rope which led to the overhanging branch.

The others watched from above as Dirk examined the sheep to make sure it had not been hurt in its fall. Then they saw their guide put the animal securely into the sling to be pulled to safety. Dirk gave a signal to Simon and his friends to pull on the rope to bring up the sheep.

Some of the boys took a firm grip on the rope and then started to pull the sheep up towards the top of the hole.

"Pull slowly," called out Dirk from the bottom of the hole as he watched the sheep move upwards.

"There's plenty of time," said Simon to the others. "We mustn't let the rope slip."

The sheep in the sling kept still as it moved through the air. It bleated once but did not struggle to try to get free. The sling did not slip as Dirk had tied it firmly to the rope. The rope was strong and the branch over which it passed did not break.

When Dirk saw that the sheep had been pulled up far enough he called out again. "Keep your grip on the rope but stop pulling," he said. "You can reach the animal now, Simon."

Simon kept one hand on the rope and reached out with the other to catch hold of the sling. He pulled this towards him to help the heavy sheep get on to the rock. As they took the sling off, it began to struggle. Then it jumped away and ran off to join the other sheep.

After Dirk had climbed out of the hole, he put the rope and canvas into his pack. In a few minutes they were all climbing up the mountain once again. Before long, the slope became much steeper and there were no more trees to be seen.

They came to a deep ravine over which they had to cross by a light, wooden bridge. A mountain stream flowed swiftly at the bottom of the ravine.

As they crossed the bridge they looked upwards at the steep cliff overhanging them. One of the boys saw something moving at the top of the cliff. He told the others and pointed to a mountain goat as it ran swiftly along.

"I didn't know that animals were to be found so far up the mountain," said John to one of his friends. "Nor did I," answered the other boy. "Look, as it runs along, the goat is making some stones fall into the ravine."

Just after the boys and girls left the bridge there was a loud noise from the cliff top. They looked up to see that a large rock was falling down the mountain side towards the wooden bridge they had just crossed.

As it ran along the cliff top, the mountain goat had dislodged a small rock. In falling, this rock had dislodged a larger rock which crashed down onto the light wooden bridge across the ravine. Dirk and his party saw part of the bridge break as the rock crashed into it. There was a brief silence and then a double splash as the rock and wood fell into the stream below.

"That just missed us!" said Simon. "One minute earlier and we would have been on the bridge as that rock hit it!"

"How are we to get back?" asked one of the girls.

"There is another way we can get back," said Dirk. "It will take longer to return that way, but we can get down in safety if we are careful. There is no need to worry about that."

Robert asked Dirk, "How will you let people know about the broken bridge?"

"We will tell the police when we return," answered the guide. "We could also have a notice put in the newspaper. Everyone will soon get to know. I expect that it will not be long before the bridge is repaired. I hope so."

Before the daylight had gone they chose a sheltered place to set up their tents for the night. As darkness fell they were safely under canvas. Most of them went to sleep quickly as they were tired.

Dirk was up early to get the breakfast, and it was not long before the others joined him. They all enjoyed their meal in the open air. At breakfast there was much talk about the exciting events of the day before. Dirk had to answer many questions about the plans for the next day.

They had a brief rest after breakfast, before they packed up their tents and other equipment. Then they were off on foot on the last part of their journey to the mountain top.

At last they safely reached the mountain peak. They stood for a few minutes looking at the wonderful view all around them, then sat down as they were tired. Although it was sunny weather and the middle of the day, it was a little cold on the mountain peak, and there was no shelter. They stayed long enough to drink some coffee they had brought with them, and for Simon to use his camera. Then they started the return journey.

"There is one difficult part of the return journey," said Dirk to Simon, as they started down the mountain side. "It's not really dangerous but we shall have to be very careful when we come to it. It is a steep cliff we have to climb down, using ropes. I wouldn't have brought your friends this way if the wooden bridge hadn't been broken by the falling rock."

Before long they came to the cliff which Dirk had described. The guide threw both ends of a long rope down the cliff and put the middle of the rope around a firm spike of rock. He then tied himself with one end of a second rope to another spike and then Simon to the other end. Everyone saw how to rope down the cliff by sliding down the doubled rope. Simon passed the rope round his body. "Hold on safely," he said to the guide with the safety rope. Then he moved over the edge and backed slowly down the cliff to the bottom.

When Simon was on the ground at the foot of the cliff he untied the rope that was round him. This was then pulled up to the cliff top and tied round John.

John slid down to join Simon. He untied the safety rope which was once again pulled up by Dirk.

Each member of the Adventure Group came down the cliff in the same way. "This really is an adventure," said one of the girls to John as she reached the ground. "Yes," replied John. "I think Simon switched on his camera just now, so some of this will be on film, to show the others at the Club."

Dirk was left at the top of the cliff. He threw down the safety rope and slid down swiftly on the doubled rope.

One of the boys asked Dirk what would happen to the doubled rope. "We will pull one end and the rope will slip round the back of the spike and fall down to us," he replied.

When they had packed the ropes Dirk was ready to continue. "Come along now. Off we go," he said.

They found it easier walking down the mountain and moved more quickly than on the journey up. However, they had a long way to go, and they had to spend one more night under canvas. This was part of the fun, and they enjoyed it.

When they reached Dirk's father's shop they telephoned the Police and a newspaper reporter to describe how the wooden bridge had been broken. Then they said goodbye to their guide and left for their own homes.

The other members of the Club were very interested to hear about the Adventure Group's week-end trip to the mountain. Simon promised to show them the colour film he had made as soon as it was ready. Meanwhile, a meeting was to be held to discuss the idea of an Open Day for the Club.

At the meeting several members said that some of their parents and friends were interested in the Club and wanted to visit it. They suggested having an Open Day for these people and any others who would like to come to see what they were doing.

Everyone thought that it was a very good idea to have an Open Day. John suggested that preparations should begin at once, and all agreed to this.

Some of the girls wanted to paint a very large coloured picture on the longest wall of the largest room. In it they planned to show as many as possible of the different activities of the Club. These would include outdoor activities as well as those that went on inside the building.

The preparations took several weeks. Meanwhile, invitations were sent out to parents, friends and other interested people.

The invitations to the Open Day at the Club included refreshments. These refreshments were prepared by the members the day before the event. By then the other preparations were finished.

Although many visitors came to the Club during the day, most people arrived during the evening. By eight o'clock all the rooms were almost filled, and there was hardly room for the Club members to move about.

There were displays of judo and dancing, and Simon showed his film of the trip to the mountain. Each of these was a great success and enjoyed by everyone. Then the people moved around the rooms, looking at the equipment of the Club and the exhibition which had been set up for them. This exhibition was of handwork by the members of the Club. Much of their handwork had been done by the girls, as the boys liked to spend more time on exercise and games. Many people were interested in the large wall painting which showed many of the outdoor activities of the Club.

While the visitors were having their refreshments, the Club leader thanked everyone for the interest they had shown. Then one of the parents, speaking for the others, thanked Simon and said that the Club was a great success.

BASKETS
BY
ANN JONES

DOLL BY
DOROTHY SE...
...AN...

New words used in this book

Total number of new words: 131